Airdrie
Marigold Library System

MAR 0 1 2018

TOOLS FOR TEACHERS

- **ATOS:** 0.6
- **GRL:** C
- **LEXILE:** 160L
- **CURRICULUM CONNECTIONS:** community helpers
- **WORD COUNT:** 77

Skills to Teach

- **HIGH-FREQUENCY WORDS:** a, can, do, I, me, my, of, us, who
- **CONTENT WORDS:** ball, book, coins, dad, friend, mom, people, read, shoes, sister, snack, sort, sum, teacher, throw, tie
- **PUNCTUATION:** periods, question marks, exclamation point
- **WORD STUDY:** long /e/, spelled ea (read, teacher), eo (people); r-controlled vowels (learn, sister); long /a/, spelled a_e (make); dipthong /oi/ (coins)
- **TEXT TYPE:** information report

Before Reading Activities

- Read the title and give a simple statement of the main idea.
- Have students "walk" though the book and talk about what they see in the pictures.
- Introduce new vocabulary by having students predict the first letter and locate the word in the text.
- Discuss any unfamiliar concepts that are in the text.

After Reading Activities

Encourage children to talk about different children in the book and the way the teacher, friend, or family member helped each of them. Then shift the discussion to things they know how to do and how they learned those skills. What did someone else teach them how to do? Have they ever taught anyone something themselves?

Tadpole Books are published by Jump!, 5357 Penn Avenue South, Minneapolis, MN 55419, www.jumplibrary.com

Copyright ©2018 Jump. International copyright reserved in all countries. No part of this book may be reproduced in any form without written permission from the publisher.

Editor: Jenny Fretland VanVoorst **Designer:** Anna Peterson

Photo Credits: Dreamstime: Petr Zamecnik, 10–11. Getty: Roy Morsch, 4–5. iStock: 8–9, 12–13. Shutterstock: Nattika, cover; ESB Professional, 1; Monkey Business Images, 6–7; Golden Pixels LLC, 14–15; Picsfive, 16tm. SuperStock: Blend Images, 2–3.

Library of Congress Cataloging-in-Publication Data is available at www.loc.gov or upon request from the publisher.
ISBN: 978-1-62031-764-8 (hardcover)
ISBN: 978-1-62031-784-6 (paperback)
ISBN: 978-1-62496-611-8 (ebook)

WHO HELPS US LEARN?

by Erica Donner

TABLE OF CONTENTS

Airdrie Public Library
111 - 304 Main Street S
Airdrie, Alberta T4B 3C3

tadpole
books

WHO HELPS US LEARN?

I can tie
my shoes.

Who helped me learn? My mom.

3

I can make a snack.

4

Who helped me learn? My sister.

I can read a book.

Who helped me learn? My teacher.

I can throw a ball.

Who helped me learn? My dad.

coins

I can sort my coins.

Who helped me learn? My friend.

I can do a sum.

sum

Who helped me learn? My teacher.

Who helps us learn?

Lots of people!

WORDS TO KNOW

ball

book

coins

shoes

snack

sum

INDEX

16